fretwork

KUHL HOUSE POETS

Mark Levine and Emily Wilson, series editors

fretwork

MICHELE GLAZER

University of Iowa Press
Iowa City

University of Iowa Press, Iowa City 52242
Copyright © 2021 by Michele Glazer
uipress.uiowa.edu
Printed in the United States of America

Design by John Laursen at Press-22

Printed on acid-free paper

Library of Congress Cataloging-in-Publication Data

Names: Glazer, Michele, author.
Title: fretwork / Michele Glazer.
Description: Iowa City: University of Iowa Press, [2021] | Series: Kuhl House Poets
Identifiers: LCCN 2021003580 (print) | LCCN 2021003581 (ebook)
           ISBN 9781609387945 (paperback) | ISBN 9781609387952 (ebook)
Subjects: LCGFT: Poetry.
Classification: LCC PS3557.L388 F74 2021 (print)
           LCC PS3557.L388 (ebook) | DDC 811/.54—dc23
LC record available at https://lccn.loc.gov/2021003580
LC ebook record available at https://lccn.loc.gov/2021003581

Acknowledgments

Thank you to Saul Melman for the cover image. Melman's *Anthropocene Series* is an ongoing project in which the artist sculpts ice into handmade paper pulp, harnessing the alchemical process of papermaking as a stage to capture materials in transition. The ice sheet splinters and begins to melt, momentarily freezing the paper pulp's semi-liquid surface. Fine carbon pigment, brushed into the resulting fissures, imprints the interaction between pulp and ice, pressure and temperature. The residual markings describe fluidity within stasis, emergence and dissolution, memory and forgetting. The artist sets a process in motion, but the materials have the last word.

I am indebted to the staff of the University of Iowa Press—Jim McCoy, Susan Hill Newton, Allison Means, Karen Copp, and Sara Hales-Brittain—and to Will Tyler for copyediting, and John Laursen for his design.

My gratitude to the editors of these periodicals in which poems first appeared, some in different form or with different titles: *Boston Review, Crazyhorse, Entropy, Iowa Review, The New Yorker, Poem-a-Day* (Academy of American Poets), *Post Road, The Volta*.

To Mary Szybist, Joanna Klink, and Ursula Irwin, my profound thanks.

I am grateful to Endi Bogue Hartigan, Brian Gard, Quigley Provost-Landrum, and Patricia Staton Thomas.

To Mark Levine and Emily Wilson, my gratitude, always.

And to John, of course.

Contents

Jean Kendall Glazer, in memory

Howard Leonard Glazer, in memory

He knew why one normally didn't look. There were too many things to see. Every feature was a forest where you'd get lost in leaves, in their serrated edges, their dim red veins, to fall through the small holes eaten by insects.

—William H. Gass, "Bed and Breakfast," *Cartesian Sonata and Other Novellas*

fretwork

Thereafter

It's the end of the world and everything's true
if you only say so.

Console yourself in knowing

little,   little flame.
We go out.

Now from the tracheae rings and loops
ornithologists gather the sound air might have made
where it gathered and moved
through acoustical cartilage—

pressing through a sequence of small rings of bone—

     the-moa the-moa   is the sound a bird made taking leave
long ago—

     Now word arrives from a distance
that the last great white rhinoceros with viable sperm has died
in san diego.

Of the two left
does it matter if they are sisters, or if one's the other's mother.

What vagueness
has overtaken us
like a slow-ripening cataract
the eyes accept.

Someone is out there

and I turn and pinch the dried pods off of hollyhock

but someone is still out there, still calling in

a quick *here kitty*

way; why answer, and why answer to that?

I turn *to* pinch, I should say.

I wheel my mother to the park

and ceding the seeds to wind

think how the years leading to the end

are no preparation for the end.

I wheeled my mother to the park; at the edge

she forgets she's mad and the chronic held hedge

of anger that sometimes erupted higher

than could be seen over for days

and days isn't there.

Yellow

                    i call & ask you are sitting in your yellow chair

                    in the kitchen waiting as usual you say to see what

                    will happen as you do now these days, for someone

                    to come, something to come clear, waiting to break

                    fast because you have had just a few sips of water

        this morning, which is not usual (it is unusually early),

                    & also not true as in accurate but true as in memory,

                    yours, of having eaten nothing & the thin

                    scree of complaint in your voice arcs in the air,

                    electrical.

i say *yellow chair* & yellow lets me recall to mind brightly not only the chair but you in it.
something has turned inside you
know there is something you
should be doing there
is no one who tells you what. it is like having yellow,   yellow!
with nothing to fix it to.

Where Ducks Sat

We sat next

And wanted to be Dutch.

If we would walk upright and not

Glance right or left the intersections

Would not come at us

Sideways, is what we thought.

But after a time it is hard

To keep feeling you are making this the best time

To look back on.

We talked. Sometimes I would walk

Past a beetle thrashing

On the rocking of its domed back and flip

It rightside. To say I'm here, and you be there.

Now the cicadas. Their long curving

Sound, and I turn

The thick line of their music into

Us. Even the ducks.

Then look back at the trip, how

Better than to be on it it is to be

Well bathed, and able to read the coins

And translate their value.

Limb

A man hauling a gunny sack

over his shoulder

as he walks, stops to break off a limb

—injuring the ornamental

cherry no taller

than he is, measured

from a distance of the earth's surface but

why measure only what you can see

                         and he inserts,

in among the other branches, with a slope of tenderness, the brokenoff one, as if

he had a right to break it, or was planting

a sapling there just to let the weight of it be held up

by the abounding livelimbs—but why wound it only to return it

to semblance? Is that it, to be above question?

Over time, leaves of the unhinged limb

will wither, drawing more attention to it

but just now it is bright daylight. We don't do much,

what can we do, who walk past him.

Competing Elegies

The service I'm not having   I'm not having at a church

but the snow, shaken   down in tufts   by small birds

whose landings flinch

the limbs

falls into itself: blue holes

in the lofted ground-snow.

                                        It is known

that what gives them this weight   is distance.

Who never wanted

anything—and there was almost nothing
she wouldn't mind
—would say

would you like
to get that for me allowing us—her children long after
we were children—
to do for her

without her
risking we might reject her,
made it a favor
she granted, this.

We'd get into it.
After a while, a week,
we'd get over it. I'll be careful
next time

not to ask she'd say.
If some day
we would feel stiffened small
for resenting her

unwillingness to want
—rather, concede
to wanting—
We didn't want her to know it. I think

about that now:
what is want that so distorts
its inhabitants?
Then she lost it. She wanted.

I tried to think that
wanting kept her alive.
She'd make a motion,
leaning forward to will a sentence into being,

picking up random
words she could reach,
and we saw there
was someone in her, barreling off, a locomotion — hopeless

we could not get inside
her there was
someone clearer, in her,
than she was.

Chapter

Christmas: the rooms lit up with tiny white lights; sparkling wine gurgles out of a suspended fountain rigged up on the kitchen island; people flirt. T and L throw the best parties.

Christmas: who's here: their friends; her clients (seeking redesign of their interiors); his; the neighborhood. Everyone could be anyone in this light, though. Footnote. Cameo. The people you see once a year live other lives too. Mixed nuts. Non-alcoholic for the children. The children. Some are carried and some have their hands up in the candy dishes and some are at the far edge of childhood, splendid in their smooth skin and bright shoes.

Bowls of salted cashews and almonds, and olives; plates of shortbread. And shrimp skewered onto wooden sticks. And dips. And crackers fanned out on trays— guests skimming the rooms are always just a few steps from something delicious. One miscarriage. Two miscarriages. They are a lovely couple. There is no invitation to the party one year that everyone looked forward to from Thanksgiving. T's new wife is pregnant and L is painting everything blue until everything she touches is hers.

Stranger

what the hagfish.

what drags up the hagfish now

& how the man says *don't touch the hagfish*

—but time's slippery & into the tank of tangled hagfish

the keeper reaches—in past

the elbow, a shoved-up

sleeve blushing with the water

wicking up

—— it's benign outside.

by *outside* I mean to leave the building with you

& enter into a *spring day* I'm asking you to imagine

the rhododendrons, the iris, mock orange in bloom, soft air, & because the danger is not visible

time turns to hagfish,

jawless & eyeless (where do I go with this?)

often I resist directness because direct mis-seizes a thing & stuns it to silence.

I imagine the particles'

drift to surfaces inhospitable, until hitch lifts them to an inhale, able

to enter another body —— it helps to think of them

as shedding

as it helps me to think of distance as

a place to meet; the distance I keep

is intended to approximate

disinterest; nothing

like the pollinators out drowsing

in the fat powdery lip while just over

there wallows another all

of them in the dry bath of pollen.

what of it? it's

what

the animal eruption sets off—

the water's sudden convulse

—much tumult of choke,

& din of the small

shaping sounds,

mouth's expiration, that hole; then to rinse

itself of the body's own off-gas it loops

& squeezing through

scrapes off such viscosity

that it may lie

   like a loose knot.

Asunder

gnats lift off the ivy bank: in

visible's back lit.

The mind that slips, and slips or so.

The nitwit night settles in,

my

Bewilderment——

I hit two / get off the /

lord, elevator

/ here

is the room

I promised her /

never to put her /

in / had

the doors close / before

me / felt

the floor I stand on rise

untroubled / hit two

/ get off

when it stops:

Everyone's there: the ones who need help

moving food to their mouths.

Also the ones who need coaxing

their mouths open:

The essay I'm reading argues that the one who is in the process
of loss is losing, *in the way the daughters of Danaus are losing*
water through their sieves. If a gerund is meant to signify ongoing
action (the essay goes on to say), what, it asks, in "missing"
is ongoing? For missing to work like losing, the one who has gone
missing must be in the gradient of disappearing. I think
how in missing
there is some one doing the missing
and there is the one being missing. How can missing
be gone and there still is a dwindling. Missing
is not a thing done.
Let missing behave like other gerunds—
you could arrest it.
But someone is missing
as she recedes. She is arranging chairs,
and spoons, and folding
and unfolding kleenex. Someone is present. She is
depopulating a pomegranate, she is removing the skin
from her thumb with her teeth, she is.

and the in   visible beats back.

It has a way of looking at you.

It has a look about it.

It has a way about it.

Not where I see it, I don't

see it. Not where I can reach my fingers in

smooth out the mess

its tangles and latches turning up the surface—

it has a way of being in your face.

It is all deranged in

cipience, all in

crementals and something set it off I want to

think there is a time

I can put a finger on that

even a small thing begins.

(The ashes have arrived, and I, failing to think of them as my mother.)

What's your name?

Michele
How do I know you so well?

o my,

you are mixed north, and mother

now to an approximate
number of sons
and daughters.

In the big room

all the fellow citizens crowd around.

A balloon

is being bobbed, they can't let it

touch the ground.

Together we are practicing expectancy.

You

who would never have tolerated silly games

like this

yet flex your wrists,

aim it my way.

I have a flat fish in my head the color of seabed.

The ocean bottom rises up—

What I had thought was rock has a mouth on it.

Pretty soon all of her chartreuses and magentas

will be worn by other residents

and she is clad in how-unlike-her

lavender.

[what] brings

to mind the mind is, mind;

what brings to

mind mind brings too —
brings tooth, the giving

in to   mind

finding its natural home there; for

closure: for

ever over
taking one whole side of it.

Hold it;

hold the bony skull as she is turned;

the head whose weight is too much;

the mouth wants;

behold the low groan;

the tongue that wants water;

flutters;

hold her head against the irreconcilable weight of it;

she is extinguishable;

she is unreachable;

she is distinguishable but no one can reach her;

she is matter;

she is not;

she will fit in a small box like an ornament

would; who would have thought.

The distended note
a warbler makes makes up
the distance where you are.

I
choke a
little.   (I am
the habit of my thoughts.)

Now you're still there. But quiet
—it is another flying thing
clearing from the throat.

enters the room

The man who enters her room to walk around it walking around picks up an object to inquire after and lays it down, and then another, and another, failing each time to find the thing that he is looking for —— (for he has only his arm by which to know the real weight of it, his palms the shape, his whole hands the texture, turning each over until he has touched every surface), making acquaintance with a merry array of objects, and all the while with a little edge of wry because the certain disapproval he holds for every object contains within it the question of why she had selected it, which weighs on him a little, or that's how she looks at it, watching him, and imagining how he would undress her, article by article, examining each part as if it were emerging from a sleeve, or bra —— that brass elephant, for instance. Sometimes he asks a question; the tile, she offers, was purchased in Amsterdam, and over there there's a clay egg the color of putty.

Trumpet Vine Takes Root

among incipient

tomato   deepunder and around

all obstacles it presses   on through packed crowded

nesses—I just   I

imagine a dry clicking—it must be

heard it must be chewed on

by something.

What is *thinking* that

in meeting matter

circumvents it?

In the fuzzy coat of hairs, the taking in and from that springing outward

into colossal light. What, or where, is upward? From there, inside, in deep

sunk windlessness, in all directions dark? What will to be

be when we are

windlessness as well. When

it has dropped its leaves it is nothing,

nothing like the animal

's sudden-falling.

Wilds

Father in dusk, in sheets, in body you
who have shrunk more than possibility

inhabit a mind I can hardly recognize as you
purport not to remember
me, your favorite,

only, daughter.

I exaggerate of course.
You don't believe me either,

little father.

What are you doing here he wants to know.
Generations of us bundle awkwardly in his head.

He promises a drive
into the green mountains.

Where's that?

It's a long story.

Diapered and drawn. My father.

one word in the onslaught.
one word in the open field at night
where he sleeps, with his glasses on,
familiar, facing the ceiling.
sits with a book open on his chest
every day to the same place.

laid out in a room intended
for dining in a bed that uplifted

the body lying in it

iknowiti knowiti knowit

now that he is
out of his mind   (and furthermore)

But yesterday he asked for cold water and pronounced it good.

You are not now
anyone you yourself
would recognize or want to have even
a casual conversation with and with it
comes a new body, fetal; and thin.

Now they zip you in to a body
bag: one size fits all.

We place white peonies on your chest.
See what you lost when you lost this world

don't go

—stranger in the hands of strangers,
dearly unfamiliar, my familiar—

in the inelegant brain
wastrel, astral, nonsense's minstrel

nothing he can do now that he does not mean to.

easy   *easy* he says meaning

not easy

stop the fucking around you ought to know that by now

tomatoes, the sungolds. just
tipping orange
enough to ripen now

last day:

the mouth still, and open now.

Stillness, be still
at the end

everyone was a moron,
bad daughter, taking notes.

not just any dead,
your father.

Clench

His toes clenched. All of him

Went into the fire. Conjure

His body empty—that sack—that final

Ruin I can't separate my father

From his body, burn it or bury

It they said you have to

Make a choice. More dark

Than I thought possible, more topo-

Graphical than thought if thought

Could be almost

Riverbed. From every direction

You are one

Long night poured into another night.

While your feet

Were still recognizable as feet I

Wanted to place

The bottoms of my own against them.

Poem of Distant Places

Hills like molting buffalo, or,

so I'm told I

take the turn off

at *Poverty Flat Road*

where the road only

ends at what it

hints at:

Dead Man Pass

are fields of wheat you could brush your hand over and be pleased.

Carry Traction Devices the signs say

in a way that wishes you, well,

a mind of ripe wheat.   Now let your body

rest, won't you

brush your hand over

this way?   Let out a green sign?

Leave me guttered?

Let me pass.

Sheep Sheep

To sleep

inside the fold.

Inside the eye

before the eyes close over

the recumbent brain:

sheep in perpetuity, in industrious wool, in surrender.

In Henry Moore's drawings the animal is depicted often with its head turned
toward the viewer; it is turned to call attention to its headness, without
which I believe the animal would not be recognizable; it would register as
a thickness that is solid but without musculature; as shipwrecked cloud.

Close the gate.

You got some ewes you want to keep some you want to cull.

It is hard to get past the sheep. They act like sheep, sheep out of the virtual gate (You've
let the sheep out, again!)

If even one sheep gets out you have to start over again, no I'm wrong.

They all move in one direction. They will act like sheep. Sheep
out of the virtual gate draw out other sheep

until you have gotten the sheep out all

but one. The most exciting moment

is sheepdog trials. Open the gate:

sometimes a red-collared sheep will beat the others out.

The sheepdog trials

are the most   Open the gate.

The bellwether bell-wearer sheep,

it looks out from its eyes at the flock: Is it any wonder that it wonders if it is

singular, or many?

On the road ahead sheep huddle marooned on a green patch in a mud field and we should stop

and we should save the sheep   but we won't.

Funk.

What's a god thing, like there's a god thing navigating?

Its head is turned at a relentless right angle to its body, looking not over but down its gun-barrel

shoulder.

Now you do it.

In the fold the sheep sleep sheep thoughts.

To be sheep is to be held in, held to, held by some other version of yourself.

Folds in the eye? No folds in the eye? Never mind
what persuades you.

I was having trouble drawing sheep and D said don't look at the legs,
draw the space between the legs.

Deep in the flock one moves counter
. . . the sheepherder shouts *bunchbunch*

but I am not here to herd.

Spring & all that

                        that part of us that
lets what grows
grow where-
ever (wants to),
          that part fists out sweet

woodruff, crowds the overly
exotic, whose little jack gleaming whitely
in the pulpit exudes
a pure cock's rebuke to the oversweet
I planted.

I planned for.

Got unruly
having to rearrange
thusly

proportions

that are not mine &

we feed them flickers.

purchased journal, c. 1932, red leather

There are the men
kitty corner, in
conversation she can't help
but overhear,

                there are accountings
of luncheons with friends, dresses
she purchases and the lengthening
suspicion that Bert's not
playing fair.
            Nobody is
writing it down
but she is.

Between altering eyelit
dresses and train wrecks the pilot's baby is kidnapped, Bert snaps at her. Isn't it a betrayal
to those who loved you to grow old.

She takes a hem out. Lets it.

Better an embolism
take her than be taken in
by him again.

. . . let me be clear
to me
why I chose her.

My smallness draws me
to her; I let it.

I rent. I let. I disavow.

Nothing happens, much; she lives there.

Issue

In the twelfth century, one hundred Cathar prisoners had their noses
cropped, their lips cut off, their eyes gouged out — then to be led by the
one man left with one eye, home to Lastours, a file of the blind, "a visible
demonstration of the ineffable mercy of God's Christian Army."
— *Cathar Castles of the Languedoc*

I would like to mention how
I hear my mother's voice rise up when she is not here.
I would like to know how

it is I hear it
but from the next room.

The real next room.
Off to one side lies my mother's death

but it is not far off,
over my shoulder, casting

a bright eye on my business. You are losing
your mind I think, leaving unhappily.

《   》

The redoubts the Cathars built issued from rock
as if they were offspring of rock, or an idea

rock had, and built.
They dragged everything they needed

up that rock including the rock
to build with; everything had to

be hauled up.
If an enemy came close

they poured hot oil down.
Oil they had hauled up.

Wood they had hauled up to heat the oil.
It worked, awhile. I would like to know how.

When she is not far off.

If I am losing it.

《 》

We have arrived at what we dread: the
diminution of loved ones, livid

and unmistakable lapses,
quick angers that lap at, lick at

dread: dread

that is the one certain shore.

《 》

I didn't share my mangoes with her so she died.

I purchased eight green mangoes to give her five and I didn't

see her before every one had ripened

so I ate them so she

died, not right then, later.

That's how it ends.

Without sweet fruit.

What happens is you fall out of sense out of order out of time.

It's a parade.

One hand cupped over
a rounded shoulder, one after
another, all the way down.

What did you see,
who got to guide
all of them home with the one
good eye?

If it's a parade be everyone, any one, and you are

from the next room

I hear *you are not*

interested in me you say *you are
not as interested in me as that other*

institution.

Truncated Sonnet

The dogs in Europe all have diarrhea. Their shit is loose sienna.

Pigeons stationed on wires swoop low & cluster

over spilt food & what they look for in this florid heat

      I'm after.

      I let you handle the map, I'll handle the gargoyles.

The sun transfixes

onto the scuffed floor inside the church geometries

of imperfection past glassmakers cast,

all of it shimmering past possession. Everywhere

I look I see through

beauty, at death. Pigeons, & pigeons.

My father: conjure him.

Peony

She. Cutting white peonies to place near his head.
She. Insisting he leave

with something sweet (the world
as water turning to stone

to be that lost
in the place he lived).

In a cave like this,
the folded hard shapes and the groaning.

The man who wouldn't eat couldn't die.
The man who couldn't die is almost pure

sound, Vivaldi
playing all the time, she thinks

to keep the mind
off his body.

She sits in some front row

crosses a leg. Adjusts a bum. Thinks of him.
Thinks music cannot be made

larger than pain.
His fine mind

a fistful of moths,

and his eyes,

and they are cousin and weary, and yellow and true.

Wigfitting

For Eliza

People will say this is the worst part about the disease
but it's not what they mean. Where in the great loss
of everything I think
does this loss fall? You,
a startled field of gossamer, now a crown
of purposeful red waves, a whatnot, why-not, (why her).

                        It is the day
the fitter will position her fingers
for a game of cat's cradle, attach the tips
to the sewed-string-ginger wigcap
and half circle a whole globe.
Flagrancy undoes its falseness. But

verisimilitude was not the goal;
the goal is Queen Elizabeth. We're not there yet.
Dress up, made up, tend and tender, pretend
and then, incline toward
extend. Through unwalled offices
I follow my friend till — we will arrive at
how we look.

The Crew, Afflicted by All It Lacks, Aimed at a Distant Star

The scientists decided that the flaw would not endanger the crew.

What's funny about that. Where is the flaw they decided against

that gives me this pause?

The bright green stick insect, how does it get across

with its short stumpy legs—the ocean is huge you

know it is not cut out for long-distance travel.

How it did cross—I consider the weight of that—

by adopting the strategy of the coconut, new research suggests.

I think how poetry is about

saying the unsayable, and am I saying it.

Flaw is soft, wearing the tongue over the sound of saying it.

Their wish that the crew complete the task is a soft fact.

In some species eggs resemble edible seeds ants gather and carry

to their comfortable, parasite-free nests where they find them

quite inedible. Follow the flaw.

The afflicted facts

speak for themselves and I would like to know how to answer.

I would like to ask the crew, who have told me

if I disconnect before they foreclose

on the landing gear, I will not lose my place

in the queue.

body

My brother grew a benign tumor in a useless organ.

You grew a tumor I said in the same language
I would use later to describe tending the tomatoes.

The thymus functions to receive the immature T cells
produced in the red bone marrow and train
them into functional mature T cells that attack
only foreign cells.

The thymus is an organ we outgrow
and then it withers. If everything
with age withers —— never
mind, I am
familiar with the foreign cell,
with the belief that a foreign cell inhabiting a body
will always be an outsider.

Inside the body is the answer to how the body moves.

With slices finer than a scalpel might render,
you think now you understand; what
do you understand
about a corpse?

At the Body Exhibit of shiny interiors
I'm invited to inspect them from multiple angles awkward
to the viewer who twists her neck and leans back to appreciate
how bodies in motion are suspended in mind,
fitted into its song-red cavity;
these bodies are real bodies I remind myself,
in poses:

> Heart Contracting
> Muscle Groups Engaging

It was so calm inside my brother
the tumor would have killed him
if he hadn't first fainted,
signaling the doctors to look inside —

a faux feint pointing
to rather than distracting from the site.

Sometimes I think a sign is just desire imposed upon the arbitrary.

Part of the job of a conductor is to point out what now is, how long now is

and when to let the held note go.

My mother at the end was a collection of parts flying in loose formation.

Never mind
that the garment of nervous system
tumbles

like a gown, in strings,
into the shape of

redress

Seen

Nature that wants to fill in

the gap the Falls

falls in and the eye falls

on: that

extends a bewildering

eye   & in its in

exact

ness —— no

less a widening

makes than what my

mind made too much

of when you

planted a tree in it.

fretwork

A rummaging—
wings on a low branch
     and scuffling
—the two crows leap back before
edging ahead again, poking,
prising the thickfist of moss—
     I can't see what I feel—
the thrill of an intelligence
humming near, for a moment,
quiets me.

Autumn is almost, is upon us.

The raptor's moth-colored wings feather
     up again, beating
back the advancing birds. The upper hand.
     The sharper beak the
bigger bird the sharper mind. Mind,
          be still.

At the opening to the   I let myself in.

     I don't know why some flowers
turn inward at night, why
     at night some leaves fold-
face into themselves. Nyctinastic
     movements are sleeping
     movements; it is the onset
  of darkness.

I let myself in.

      The orange geum—brilliant, flat-
blossomed—the elsewhere
    hummingbird vibrates above it
before flitting
    off to top itself off on
a blossom-shape more
     appropriate.

You are out of reach,
       I am out of sorts,
   and the crows
     are at it again, ruckusing
now in the high gingko, or
       just looking around
  and when it's time they take off
     a hurl of crows   isn't it something
  to have nothing
      to do with us
    wouldn't we be better
  beside the point.

Path of Totality

I caught wind of rains.

I watch the sun

get bitten into   and as it goes

                        across the river

        the cow chokes on a weed

—the green weeds.

The cow as they enter her.

The light here

is inconclusive.

We are inconclusive. A small event

in the bull's eye

of the path the moon

tracks, lugging its shadow along behind it.

In perspective, you stand in relation

to what you are looking at;

                      I thought I could hold

that moment at the edge of totality,

after the last desultory breath

and before the profound absence.

I wanted to.

The day was made longer by the shadow
folding itself over a folded
landscape of shallow-bellied rivers and

I thought I could position myself at the tautline
where the moon slipped in like a habit
to cover the sundisk. The birds

quieted.
Of the sun—

I wonder, is it a relief
to have something

between you
and all these sad worshippers?

Where does a gaze end when there is nothing to stop it.

Notes

"Asunder": On the grammar of missing, I am indebted to Michael D. Snediker's review of Dara Wier's collection of poems, *You Good Thing*. Snediker's review, "Lost and (Almost) Found," was published in the *Boston Review*, September 18, 2013.

"Issue": The Châteaux de Lastours, four stone towers built high on crags in the southwest corner of France, were redoubts of the Cathars, whose religious tenets were in conflict with those of the Catholic Church, and whose increasing popularity with the populace made them a target. In 1208 Pope Innocent III launched a crusade against them. "Here at the isolated Lastours castles . . . the Cathars spent much of 1209 heroically fending off the onslaught. So the crusader leader, the sadistic Simon de Montfort, resorted to primitive psychological warfare. He ordered his troops to gouge out the eyes of one hundred luckless prisoners, cut off their noses and lips, then send them back to the towers led by a prisoner with one remaining eye." (Tony Perrottet, "The Besieged and the Beautiful in Languedoc," *The New York Times*, May 6, 2010.)

"body": Body Worlds is a traveling exhibition of human bodies preserved through plastination, then dissected and displayed in order to show anatomical structures and organs. The accompanying text states that its purpose is educational, to inform viewers about anatomy, physiology, and health. Many of the bodies are presented in motion or in familiar poses, such as riding a bicycle or sitting bent over a chessboard.

Kuhl House Poets

Christopher Bolin
Ascension Theory

Christopher Bolin
Form from Form

Shane Book
Congotronic

Oni Buchanan
Must a Violence

Oni Buchanan
Time Being

Michele Glazer
fretwork

Michele Glazer
On Tact, & the Made Up World

David Micah Greenberg
Planned Solstice

Jeff Griffin
Lost and

John Isles
Ark

John Isles
Inverse Sky

Aaron McCollough
Rank

Randall Potts
Trickster

Bin Ramke
Airs, Waters, Places

Bin Ramke
Matter

Michelle Robinson
The Life of a Hunter

Vanessa Roveto
bodys

Vanessa Roveto
a women

Robyn Schiff
Revolver

Robyn Schiff
Worth

Sarah V. Schweig
Take Nothing with You

Rod Smith
Deed

Donna Stonecipher
Transaction Histories

Cole Swensen
The Book of a Hundred Hands

Cole Swensen
Such Rich Hour

Tony Tost
Complex Sleep

Pimone Triplett
Supply Chain

Nick Twemlow
Attributed to the Harrow Painter

Susan Wheeler
Meme

Emily Wilson
The Keep